In Progress

Bekah Concoby

BookLeaf
Publishing

India | USA | UK

Presentation by *BookLeaf Publishing*

Web: www.bookleafpub.com

E-mail: info@bookleafpub.com

ISBN: 978-93-5744-458-3

First edition 2022

ACKNOWLEDGEMENT

A huge "thank you" goes out to everyone who ever encouraged me to continue writing. My parents, my brothers, my husband, Anna, Ruth, Jordyn, Kyra, Kaitlyn, and countless Language Arts teachers (especially Mr. Christensen) have all been a part in getting me to where I can finally say, "Look! I wrote a book!!!"

Who Am I?

It should be a basic question to answer:
"Who are you? What do you do?"
I could give you my name,
My hobbies,
My interests,
The things I like to do when time stalls,
But that only tells you a fragment.
If you were willing to listen,
I could tell you my fears,
My dreams,
My humor,
The kind of person I want to be someday,
And more.
If you still stayed, I could tell you more
About what has shaped me to be where I am,
The good,
The bad,
The ugly,
The things I rejoice in,
The things I regret,
And that's great.
But there's a problem there, isn't there?
Because, you see,
Asking me who I "am"
Implies a state of being,

And beings are always in flux.
Those things that I could tell you today
Aren't the same as what I would've told you
A month ago,
A year ago,
Three years ago.
Sometimes, what I would say today
Was not what I would've said yesterday.
And, I think that this the most beautiful thing
about humanity,
That we never stop.
The bad habits we fall into, we can fall out of,
The bad people in our lives can be removed,
The bad things we think and say can be changed,
If we try.
We are always beings
In progress.
I call it "progress", because I choose to believe
That we are always working towards something
Better.

Golden Afternoons

Somedays, when

I
Push open the sliding glass doors,
The warm, glowing sun seems to

Melt
In the sky,
Leaving soft embers in glittered trails.
It is warm, soft and safe.

Here
The light is gold,
Luminescent,

And
It's easy to see
Why time stops and
Stares for a moment.
The leaves leave metal medallions
Of shimmered color

Here
And there, dappling the grass.
The whispering wind calls, and

        I
Can't help but answer back,
Pouring my soul into the daydream.
Butterflies, large and small,
Bring treasure to show me,
Though the true gems lie
In the stained glass wings that carry them
Across opal and sapphire skies ,
Not the precious stones they

        Find
When the birds, woven of twigs and bark,
Stop their sweet songs just long enough
To ask me to tell them a story
Of life and laughter,
I tell them again and again that, for

        Myself
Each day is a new story,
If you just look for it.
Then, once the sun has melted
Past the mountains proud,
And the sky has begun to pull
Curtains of stars over its broad face,
Time has again begun its course.
The stars twinkle and gleam, and,
In ancient voices,
Thank me for coming today,

And if I will please, please come

      Again.
I'll be back tomorrow,
I promise,
With a new story to tell.

To My Future Daughter

Things have changed a lot since I last wrote a
poem like this,
But my wish for you has never changed.
Daughter dearest, my hope, my dream for you
Is that you don't grow up too fast.
I hope you never get tired of running through the
grass with bare feet,
I pray you never stop dreaming of what it might
be like to fly.
When darkness comes, grasping
With blackened claws of doubt,
And sharpened teeth of despair,
To steal your magic,
I will fight it off as long as I can so that you
Can keep chasing after fairies and dragons.
Whether you learn to love books, or video
games,
Or TV shows,
Those characters will be your friends when I
cannot be,
And I think you will find that you are never
Alone

With your imagination to keep you company.
So don't grow up too fast, my dear one,
Keep breathing life into fantasy,
Because one day you will wake up,
And a Dragon Rider's sword will be a stick in
your hand,
And a bird kid's feathered wings will disappear
into nothing.
Until then,
May the magic you've created
Light your every step
And fill every golden afternoon with wonder.
Don't grow up too fast,
please.

Words

I have, on a number of occasions,
Found out the hard way
That if you love someone, you should tell them
as often as you can
Because you don't know when your last chance
to say it will be.
So, my husband, although I know you know
I'm going to keep saying it, as often as I can.
See, in the past, when I loved a boy,
I would fill pages and pages of notebooks
Using my words and imaginations to
Run films in my head of what could be,
Idealizing and hoping and dreaming,
My heart guiding my pen,
And yet, I never told any of those boys.
I could never get out those three words.
I think I was saving them, without really
meaning to,
Until I found the right person.
And yet, once I found you,
I realized that I didn't need all those extra words,
I didn't need poems to fill in the pieces of the
pictures
I wanted to paint.
Every time I say it to you,

It means so, so much more than notebooks
Could ever say.
I hope you don't get tired of hearing me say it,
Because I'll never get tired of saying
"I love you."

The Meaning of Love

Since I was a child, I have always believed in
God
But, as I grew older, I came to realize
That it is one thing to believe He is real,
And another to believe that He is my Father.
He sometimes seems so far away, and distant.
It wasn't until a friend's poem about how he
loves

His children, opened my eyes to how God loves
Us, for if "Dad" can mean "love", and God is a
Father,
Then God means love, too, and the word and the
feeling
Of absolute adoration that a father feels for his
children
Cannot be separated. If loved ones make us
smile,
Imagine how He smiles down at us, His
children, below.

Some days, I feel like I'm below
Anyone and everyone, like I'm worthless and
stupid
And like any effort I make falls pitifully short of
what I
Should be doing, what I should be. And on those
days
Of anger and sadness and silent tears hidden in
closets,
I have to stop and look. The trees. The sea. The
stars.

He made beauty. In the stillness of the stars,
He whispers songs of peace. He made all of this
for us. I know
That it is hard to live those days of rage and
regret,
Of abuse and anxiety, of fear and failure, of
helpless hopelessness
And call that "love." The person I love most
Had a wretched childhood, a broken home,

And he chooses each day to build a new home,
To break the cycle, and to let Heavenly Father
Carry him through his past. God will not use
trials and
Tribulation as punishment or retribution, but as a
tool to teach us,

If we are humble enough to learn. When my
strength is insufficient,
When my stamina breaks, it is holy to know that
I can call upon His name.

As we have heard over and over, there is power
in a name,
And I think it shows much that, out if all the
names He could have chosen,
Creator, Master, Lord and Ruler, Omniscient
God,
The one that He has chosen for us to call Him by
is
"Father." I think, someday, we will look back
and be amazed
At how intricately He was involved in our lives.
He is Love, and He is God.

My Father, my God, is perfectly aware of and
loves
His children below, and He who places the stars
Carefully in their home is He who knows my
name.

On Loss

It's okay to miss her.
It's okay to be sad, and to cry.
It's okay to hurt.
It's okay to be angry.
It's okay to scream and yell,
It's okay to be conflicted.
Or to just be numb.
It's okay to take your whole life to move on,
It's okay to bury the pain and keep moving.
But when the roaring and the weeping are done,
Be sure to thank God for
Each and every day that she was there.
We carry the pieces of those we love with us
even after they're gone,
And sometimes the best we can do
Is be grateful that a piece of us
Came from someone
So wonderful.

Pieces

Every time I walk under a doorway, I reach up
and hit the top.
It was something I copied from a best friend,
And something I keep alive even after
Our feet don't grace those high school halls.
Whenever I braid my hair,
(Which is a lot, to be honest),
I remember that time I was with Ruth,
And a boy I had never spoken to
Asked us to teach him how to braid,
So he could help his mother
Who was losing the use of her hands.
I remember teasing a young man in college
For always texting me back past midnight,
And now I do exactly the same.
Whenever I wear my hair pulled back,
I have to smile at the memory
Of a sweet old lady
Who told me I was one of the few people
Who could pull off having all my hair pulled
back.
I still do my eyebrows the way Katie showed
me,
I still make cookies the way Matt taught me
The one day I showed up to his house,

Determined to cheer him up,
And I still write stories, with thoughts of Libby
Racing through my head.
I am a composite being,
Carrying pieces of the things I've been taught,
Or shown,
Or valued.
Granted, not every piece is good.
I remember every negative comment,
Or insult I've received,
And some days, those shape me
Just as much
Or more,
As the good does.
But, I am proud to carry the good pieces
Of those good people,
And many of them will never know how much
they shaped me.
I hope that someone somewhere
May cherish the good pieces of me.

Memories

Tuck my head down lower,
Don't look into their eyes.
Stop the words inside my head,
Stop the doubt.
Put in my earphone,
Escape to the reality that I have shaped,
Not the one that shapes me.
Pretend I'm alright,
Pretend I can talk to you without feeling shaky,
Pretend I don't go home and pick apart our
conversations,
Wishing I could be better.
Pretend my hands were still as I typed my
number into your phone,
Pretend I can just talk to the people in my
classes without being nervous,
Pretend there isn't a constant worry in the back
of my mind.
Pretend I don't wait until someone else throws
away their tray so I know it's okay for me to,
Pretend I don't say anything in class because I'm
too smart, or disinterested, not because I'm
afraid of bringing attention to myself.
Smile like I feel confident in who I am,

Smile at everyone I see, because what I need
most in the world is for someone to smile at me.
Be kind because the world needs more kindness,
Be kind because all I want is someone to notice
me, maybe I must notice them first.
Hold my breath because there's so much feeling
inside, and yet I feel nothing,
And yet I am where I am because I feel too
much
Be flustered, be shy, be hesitant, glance up from
under my eyelashes, smile not too wide,
It is easier to be adorably awkward and timid
than fragile.
Pretend I am confident,
Pretend I am strong.
Pretend I am something better than these broken
parts:
Tuck my head down lower,
Don't look into their eyes.
Put in my earphone,
Run away to a place I feel safe inside my own
skin.
Stop the words inside my head,
Stop the doubt,
And breathe.

Photograph

When she ripped up that photograph, she had
wanted it gone
Destroyed
Erased
Whatever
She wanted to scour him out of her heart
Just like he had scoured her out of his life
She didn't want to carry those memories.

A few days later, she stands over a casket
Silently
Weeping
The pieces in her hand
It had never occurred to her that she might never
have the chance
To make memories with him again
She scatters the fragments over the body
And buries the memories with him.

Answers

I don't have all the answers
Somedays, I wish I did.
It would be a whole lot easier that way.
I wish I could tell you the exact reason why
There is pain and sickness and suffering
In your life
In my life
In every life
I wish I could tell you in advance
Some of the positive things that can come
From such things,
Like compassion,
Understanding,
Maybe the ability to help someone going
through the same circumstances.
I wish that would make it okay.
Light at the end of the tunnel
Doesn't make the tunnel any less
Scary,
But it does make the trip a bit brighter,
If only a bit.
I wish I could carry you through your tunnels,
And sometimes, I wish you could carry me
through mine.
I wish I had the answers you seek,

But answers are best seen in hindsight.
I hope, someday, that you may look back
And smile,
If only a bit.

When the Words Won't Come

Sometimes, the noise in my head become
So loud
I can barely think.
Trying to form a coherent sentence
Comes sluggishly, a thousand
Fragments trying to
Form something real.
Usually, I can put the words on paper,
A stream of consciousness
From my heart to
My hand,
From pen to
Paper,
But in times like that, the
Words just
Stop.

I think that these are the moments when
God loves me the most,
When I am on my knees,
With an unspoken need,
Something too Much

To put into words,
And the words won't come.
He understands
What I physically am
Unable to say
Until the storm calms,
And the fragments start
To piece themselves
Back together.

Someday

Someday,
It will
All be okay.
Things look bad sometimes
That's just the way life
Goes sometimes, and it's not your
Fault that bad things happen to you.
When you're ready to get out
Of the rut you're stuck
Let me know.
You'll get there.
You'll be
Okay.

Love You

Try not to dwell too much
On the pain you left in the past.
The past can stay where it is, because
Home is where you make it.
Everyone carries with them some
Memories they wish they could leave behind
Only, you have learned to carry them like armor
Of steel and bone.
Nothing can erase those scars
And like a poorly healed injury
Nothing could really heal the past but break it
again.
Damage so old is hard to heal. But,
Believe me when I say I would carry you
All the way back to heaven itself, because only
Someone higher than I
Can perform that kind of healing, and help you
see the
King you were always meant to be.

The Secret to Peace

This world is a place of unrest,
Of violent intolerance.
Skin color, religion, nationality, gender,
sexuality, political stance,
There is so much that people choose to get mad
about.
For lack of a better way to say it,
I don't get it.
People have differences,
And thank heavens!
Can you imagine how bland and boring the
world would be
If we were all cookie-cutter,
Copy-and-paste humans?
Society thrives on differences,
On diversity,
And yet makes any differences
Undesirable.
Now, I don't agree with everything everyone
says,
I don't approve of some lifestyles,
But I can disagree without
Enforcing my idea of right or wrong.
I don't have the right to tell anyone

That they are wrong for living how they want to
live,
Anymore than they have the right to call me
wrong.
I don't understand how a difference of opinion
Equals violence.
Maybe I'm foolish,
Or naive,
But I truly believe that the good in people
Far outweighs
Any choice they make that I may or may not
agree with.
I believe that it's really that simple.

Monsters

She knew there were monsters.
She was only a little girl,
But still she knew it.
There had been one in her closet,
One under the stairs,
One that lurked behind the fridge and hissed all
night long.
But, one day, they all vanished.
Then, the Monster under her bed appeared.
It never did anything, it barely moved,
But every time she dared to peek underneath her
bed,
It was always looking back at her with huge red
eyes
The size of her fist.
Her parents could never see it,
As soon as the light flicked on,
The Monster vanished,
And so, after weeks, she gave up.
So she waited for the Monster to do…
Something. Anything.
But it never did.
One night, she grew angry,
Tired and sick of the endless fear,
And so she rolled to the edge of the bed

And peered down,
Staring right at the huge red eyes,
And demanded, "Why are you here?!"
To her horror, she watched an enormous
Mouth of teeth shape itself into the shape of a
smile,
And a raspy, metallic voice said, "Little girl…"
She threw herself backwards, screaming,
And long, skeletal gray fingers wrapped
themselves
Over the edge of the bed
As the Monster started to lift itself up.
Her parents came running,
But the moment the lights turned on,
The fingers were gone,
And there were no eyes or teeth underneath the
bed.
A few minutes after her parents had left,
The girl heard the voice again:
"Little girl…"
This time, she waited, whimpering,
As the Monster slowly and carefully
Unfolded its long body from under her bed.
Upon seeing its terrible face and hideous form,
She couldn't hold back the screams again.
Again, her parents came and checked for
A Monster who seemed to not exist,
And left her alone again.
After an impossibly long wait,

Where the girl lay curled in her blanket,
Shivering in fear,
The voice came again:
"Little girl…"
But this time, it was hesitant,
And the Monster did not try to stand up
Or leave underneath her bed.
"Little girl…"
Although the voice was harsh and metallic,
It was also surprisingly gentle.
There was no malice in the voice
From under her bed.
"Little girl… I am here
To keep the darkness safe for you.
I chase away the monsters who want to hurt you,
And I keep out the Things outside.
You see, little girl…"
Its voice began to fade as the first morning ray
hit her curtains,
"Not all Monsters are monsters…"

Change Begins Here

Sunrise only matters
Once the night has come,
When the stars have risen;
Yesterday's sun called home.

Light only has meaning
Once the darkness has spoken.
It breaths soft soothing words
To heal what Night has broken.

Dawn only can happen
Once silence has fallen.
Only then can it whisper colors
And sounds to answer its calling.

Wistfully

He sits and lets the world pass by
He is quiet, doesn't say much.
He watches the stars in the sky,
And wishes, somehow, that he could fly
But I know clouds are for dreams, not touch.

He wanders down a lonely street,
He is light gray, a shade below white.
His sound is a slow, empty beat,
Watching only his own feet,
He is made of shadows and light.

But random things will make him rise -
A word, a touch, a voice, a scent,
An askance glance, looks of surprise,
The light reflected in warm eyes -
And I am in the past again.

He is thoughtful, and rather kind,
Though some find him foolish, folly,
Still he is of a gentle mind.
Look in deep, and you just may find,
Your own quiet Melancholy.

THEN/NOW

Theater / Psychology
Reading and writing / TV shows
Cheerful / Quiet and thoughtful
Hesitant / Affectionate
Fearful / Still fearful, but wiser now
Terrified of the future / Comfortable in not knowing
Flawed / Willing to become better
For Good or Bad, I am not permanent.

Scars

Some have scars on their fingers and hands that
tell
Happy stories of accidents and stupid mistakes.
Some have scars on their wrists that tell
A less cheerful narrative.
Some have scars on their arms and shoulders,
some that talk
Of surgeries or car accidents, or just
Friends messing around that ended badly.
Scarred knees might tell of a clumsy girl
Who manages to find anything that could be the
slightest bit sharp,
Scarred ribs speak of a boy who should have
died when he was young,
But the miracle of medicine saved his life.
Some scars are the saga of a person who had
been strong too long.
Some are from the best of times,
Some are from the worst of times,
But one way or another,
They are the story of a fighter.

Tomorrow

Night falls slowly,
So gradual that sometimes,
You miss it until it has
Come.
The noise of the day grows
Quiet
And all the tension finds a chance to
Ease.
It's a good time to tidy,
Sweeping up cobwebs and bad news,
Dusting off dirt and depression,
Scraping away gunk and fear,
Mopping up filth and tears,
Putting away dishes and anxieties,
Until the clutter and your mind are
Clear.
Throw away the unwanted things -
Take the bad parts of today -
Gather the things that happened that you're not
proud of -
Let it all be tomorrow's problem.

Tomorrow is another day...

Layers

One of the most beautiful things
About humanity
Is that it is not face value.
People have layers,
To be cliche, "like an onion",
And yet thus it is.
Once you get through
The top layer
Of my shyness that
Presents itself as intimidatingly
As it can,
Then you reach the sunshine layers.
These are warm
And kind and happy
And find joy in the moment.
They are playful
And loving
And live life to its fullest.
If you manage to peel back those layers,
You'll start to find duller layers
Of self doubt and insecurity
Anxiety expressing itself in fear.
Past that lay the darkest layers
Of depression
And resentment

And sometimes anger.
When you reach the core?
Honestly, I'm not sure what's there.
I have my theories,
But ultimately, I choose to believe that it's
something
Good,
Like the sunshine layers.
Maybe, with enough time,
The sunshine in the outer layer,
And the warmth from whatever is the core,
Will be able to brighten those darker layers in
between.
I really don't know
What the whole picture of me
Looks like.
But I take comfort in the knowledge
That a snapshot of who I am now
Is not the final product.
I have time to become better,
To become
More.